Create a  30 Day Challenge
for Your Audience

Boost Your Business by Sharing
Your Knowledge and Expertise

D'vorah Lansky, M.Ed.

An Action Guide for Authors

Vibrant Marketing Publications
Hartford, CT

Published by Vibrant Marketing Publications
Copyright ©2017 D'vorah Lansky

www.ActionGuidesForAuthors.com

ISBN 978-0-9967431-7-4

Dedication

This book is dedicated to the amazing participants of our
Create a Challenge Experience program.

Your dedication to helping your audience, by
providing them with a transformative
challenge experience, is inspiring!

Here's to your success!
D'vorah

Table of Contents

Table of Contents

Introduction

Offering a challenge experience to your audience will provide you with many benefits! You'll be able to grow your list of email subscribers, boost your book and product sales, and develop relationships with members of your target audience.

In this workbook, you have access to a step-by-step approach to designing, creating, marketing, and launching an amazing challenge experience for your audience. When you offer your students and clients a challenge experience, you'll want them to go through the training and take action. That said, you'll want to lead by example by applying yourself to going through the training and action steps provided to you in this workbook.

Here are some tips to help you make the most of this opportunity:

- ○ Schedule time to go through the workbook and apply what you learn.
- ○ Know that wherever you are, in the process of planning, marketing or conducting your challenge, you are in the perfect place! The key is to keep the momentum going and celebrate accomplishments along the way.
- ○ Embrace this opportunity and you'll reap the rewards.

Congratulations again on your decision to create a challenge experience for your audience. Before you know it, you'll be welcoming participants to your program!

I look forward to sharing this content with you and look forward to celebrating the launch of your challenge experience. Please email me once your challenge is ready to launch, as you may be featured in our Challenge Showcase. ReachMoreReaders.com/support

Here's to Your Success!

Challenge Experience Examples
From Our Course Participants

CreateAChallengeExperience.com

From Sorrow to Serenity: 21 Steps from Grief to Peace
Uma Girish, Grief Guide and Dream Coach, UmaGirish.com

Challenge Description: My program offers simple daily steps that help move grieving folks from the space of overwhelm, indecisiveness, and a lack of focus to a space of clarity, focus, and renewal. I have 3 modules: Body, Mind, Spirit. Each module is 7 days long. On each day I will offer a simple new tip for my audience to begin the journey toward wellness and healing. My participants are grieving a loss, whether it is the death of someone they love, the end of a relationship, an empty nest, a parent's dementia, or a lack of purpose and meaning in their lives. Through this challenge, they will be able to take a simple step every single day, for 21 days, to move toward peace, focus and a sense of empowerment.

Manage Your Career Crisis with Ease
Bette Novak, Executive Career Coach, BetteNovak.com

Challenge Description: The first 7 days of my Challenge will use exploratory and self-discovery tools and questionnaires to answer questions such as; "Where am I in my career?" and "Does my career make me fulfilled?" During that time, we'll learn 5 directions that a successful career can take and what are the pros, the cons and the outdated beliefs that people have in managing and moving their careers when they are dissatisfied, feel a need for a change, fell overwhelmed, or don't want to work in the same organization or company anymore. From there we will move into a 14 day paid program.

Devotions of His Love 7 Day Challenge
Mary Jones, Minister, PreludeToaJourney.com

Challenge Description: For 7 days we'll embark on a journey where participants will experience a greater expression of love in their relationship with God through the discipline of daily devotions. For some, it will be a refreshing time of revitalization. Participants will receive an email every other day with that day's challenge. This Challenge will prepare participants for a greater challenge of writing their own devotions for Sunday school, bible study and worship and personal growth.

Challenge Experience Examples
From Our Course Participants

CreateAChallengeExperience.com

21 Day Best Cellular Nourishment Plan with Barley Max
Isabel Richli, Health and Weight Loss Coach, LadyJeunesse.com

Challenge Description: This is a free challenge for my Barley Max clients. I'll also promote it as a free opt-in gift to build my email list and build a relationship with my list. Participants will experiment with new habits for health and weight loss. The content will be delivered via email, over 21 days. Participants will discover an easy way to drink a daily green juice that fully nourishes their bodies.

7 Day Healthy Habits Challenge
Trish Dennison, Health and Happiness Coach, TrishDennison.ca

Challenge Description: My participants want to live healthy but don't know where to begin. They are unaware of simple health basics that can make a huge difference. The goal of this challenge is to bring conscious awareness to their present patterns as they begin to implement simple healthy habits; drinking more water, deep belly breathing, stress checking the body, tracking their sugar and carbohydrate intake, learning about the standard essential vitamins needed and creating a routine for consistency, paying attention to their thoughts and subsequent feelings, keeping a gratitude list and questioning what their next goal is. Through this challenge they will begin to feel better, become aware of unconscious habits and be open and eager to learn what they can do next.

7 Day Divorce Courage Building Challenge For Women
Lisa McNally, Divorce Coach, DivorceCourageBuildingChallengeForWomen.com

Challenge Description: Divorce isn't easy. It can be quite overwhelming. This challenge experience is designed to help divorcing and divorced women develop the courage they need to make the decisions necessary to improve any aspect of their lives with complete confidence, clarity and control. Participants will receive: daily workbook/journaling exercises based on journaling prompts, daily thought-provoking, courage-building homework exercises/assignments, daily courage-building affirmations, daily private Facebook group check-ins, two live group coaching calls with me and a teleseminar training session.

Possible Topics for Challenge Experiences

Looking at a list of possible challenge topics, can help generate ideas for a challenge topic for your audience. As you read through these lists, check off items of interest and scroll down to the blank section to jot down ideas, as they come to mind.

Health Based Challenges

- ○ Cut Out the Sugar Challenge
- ○ Daily Exercise Challenge
- ○ Go to the Gym Challenge
- ○ Green Smoothie Challenge
- ○ Low Carb Challenge
- ○ Meditation Challenge
- ○ Walking Challenge
- ○ Get More Sleep Challenge

Challenges for Authors

- ○ Book Cover Design Challenge
- ○ Book Editing Challenge
- ○ Book Marketing Challenge
- ○ Book Study Challenge
- ○ Book Writing Challenge
- ○ Character Development Challenge
- ○ Teach Your Book Challenge
- ○ Video Trailer Challenge

Internet Marketing Challenges

- ○ Blogging Challenge
- ○ List Building Challenge
- ○ Social Networking Challenge
- ○ Podcasting Challenge
- ○ Audio or Video Postcard Challenge
- ○ Online Interviews Challenge
- ○ Video Creation Challenge
- ○ Web Graphics Challenge

Challenges D'vorah Has Created

- ○ 90 Day Power Plan
- ○ Book Marketing Challenge
- ○ Course Creation Challenge
- ○ Create a Challenge Experience
- ○ List Building Challenge for Authors
- ○ Podcasting Challenge
- ○ Productivity Challenge
- ○ Virtual Book Tour Challenge

Our Course Members' Challenge Topics

- ○ Sleep and Relaxation Challenge
- ○ Living with Purpose Challenge
- ○ Emotional Wellness Challenge
- ○ Worksite Wellness Challenge
- ○ Manuscript Momentum Challenge
- ○ Write a Nonfiction Book Challenge

Your Topic Area:

- ○ _____
- ○ _____
- ○ _____
- ○ _____
- ○ _____
- ○ _____

Capture Challenge Ideas That You Discover

The *Challenge* concept is becoming popular in every area of life and business and more and more challenge opportunities are popping up. Use the sections below to capture challenge topics, concepts and formats you come across which intrigue you.

Challenge Title: _____

What intrigues you about this challenge? _____

_____

What, about how this challenge is being offered, would you like to draw from when creating your challenge? _____

_____

Challenge Title: _____

What intrigues you about this challenge? _____

_____

What, about how this challenge is being offered, would you like to draw from when creating your challenge? _____

_____

Challenge Title: _____

What intrigues you about this challenge? _____

_____

What, about how this challenge is being offered, would you like to draw from when creating your challenge? _____

_____

Capture Challenge Ideas That You Discover

The *Challenge* concept is becoming popular in every area of life and business and more and more challenge opportunities are popping up. Use the sections below to capture challenge topics, concepts and formats you come across, which intrigue you.

Challenge Title: _____

What intrigues you about this challenge? _____

_____

What, about how this challenge is being offered, would you like to draw from when creating your challenge? _____

_____

Challenge Title: _____

What intrigues you about this challenge? _____

_____

What, about how this challenge is being offered, would you like to draw from when creating your challenge? _____

_____

Challenge Title: _____

What intrigues you about this challenge? _____

_____

What, about how this challenge is being offered, would you like to draw from when creating your challenge? _____

_____

Capture Challenge Ideas That You Discover

The *Challenge* concept is becoming popular in every area of life and business and more and more challenge opportunities are popping up. Use the sections below to capture challenge topics, concepts and formats you come across, which intrigue you.

Challenge Title: _____

What intrigues you about this challenge? _____

_____

What, about how this challenge is being offered, would you like to draw from when creating your challenge? _____

_____

Challenge Title: _____

What intrigues you about this challenge? _____

_____

What, about how this challenge is being offered, would you like to draw from when creating your challenge? _____

_____

Challenge Title: _____

What intrigues you about this challenge? _____

_____

What, about how this challenge is being offered, would you like to draw from when creating your challenge? _____

_____

Notes

Section One

Identify the Perfect Challenge Topic for Your Audience

Activities
1-6

The first step in creating your challenge experience is to get clear on who your audience is, what they are interested in, what you'd love to teach, and what your areas of expertise are.

The activities in this section will help you to get clear on the above and help you to identify the perfect challenge topic for your audience.

Define Your Challenge Creation Goals

Today's action step is to get clear on your "why" for wanting to offer a challenge experience. You'll also have the opportunity to give thought to how you and your audience can benefit from your challenge.

Getting clear on your "why" will provide you with motivation and inspiration for creating a challenge experience for your audience. To begin, give some thought to what your "why" is for wanting to create a challenge experience. Turn to the facing page and complete the suggested activities. Getting clear on your "why" will fuel your passion for creating your challenge.

At the end of the day, journal your accomplishments in the section provided below. By prioritizing time to take action and reflect on your activity and results each day, you'll maximize the benefits you'll receive from this opportunity.

What I Accomplished Today

Activity #1 - Action Steps
What is Your "Why" for Creating a Challenge

Knowing what your why is and what your goals are will help to create a laser focus for your challenge experience.

What is your "why" for wanting to create a challenge for your audience?

_____

_____

_____

How will you benefit by offering a challenge? _____

_____

_____

_____

How will your audience benefit by participating in your challenge? _____

_____

_____

_____

What are your hopes for your program? _____

_____

_____

_____

Activity #2

Give Thought to Who Your Niche Audience Is

Today's action step is to identify your niche audience. By knowing who your ideal audience is, you'll be able to develop relationships with those who want and need what you have to offer. This creates a win/win situation.

Turn to the next page and spend some time identifying who your target audience is. This is essential as it will allow you to maximize your efforts and your results while helping the exact people who need what you have to offer. Once you've identified your niche audience, it will be easy for you to design and create a challenge experience that they can benefit from.

At the end of the day, journal your accomplishments in the section provided below. By prioritizing time to take action and reflect on your activity and results each day, you'll maximize the benefits you'll receive from this opportunity.

What I Accomplished Today

Activity #2 - Action Steps

Identify Your Niche Audience and Ideal Student

Knowing who your ideal audience is and thus who your ideal student is, will serve you well as you begin to design and create your challenge experience.

Describe your ideal student: _____

_____

_____

_____

List common demographics, life experiences or attributes of your ideal student.

_____   _____

_____   _____

_____   _____

What do they want most? _____

_____

_____

_____

What else can you share, that would help you to identify your niche audience?

_____

_____

_____

Activity #3

Identify What Solution Your Audience Seeks

Today's action step is to identify the challenges and obstacles your audience seeks a solution to. By providing them with a challenge experience that offers a solution to what they struggle with, you'll be helping a lot of people while growing your email list and building your business.

Turn to the next page for today's exercise. Once you identify the interests, challenges, and desires of your audience, you'll be paving the way to identifying the perfect topic for your challenge experience.

At the end of the day, journal your accomplishments in the section provided below. By prioritizing time to take action and reflect on your activity and results each day, you'll maximize the benefits you'll receive from this opportunity.

What I Accomplished Today

Activity #3 - Action Steps

Identify What Solutions Your Audience Seeks

Create a list of your ideal student's interests, struggles, and desires.

What are they most interested in?

- _____
- _____
- _____
- _____
- _____

What do they struggle with most?

- _____
- _____
- _____
- _____
- _____

What do they want to achieve or learn more about?

- _____
- _____
- _____
- _____
- _____

Date: _____

Describe Your Areas of Expertise

Today's action step is to write about your strengths and areas of expertise. As you develop the idea for your challenge, you want to be clear about what it is you offer and who it is you serve. This makes for a powerful formula for success.

What have you experienced or studied that your audience would love to learn? There are people who are eager to know how to accomplish what comes naturally to you. Take this into account, along with the wants and needs of your target audience, as you identify the topic for your challenge.

At the end of the day, journal your accomplishments in the section provided below. By prioritizing time to take action and reflect on your activity and results each day, you'll maximize the benefits you'll receive from this opportunity.

What I Accomplished Today

Activity #4 - Action Steps

List Your Interests and Areas of Expertise

Describe your areas of expertise: _____

_____

_____

_____

What interests do you have that complement your expertise?

- ○ _____
- ○ _____
- ○ _____
- ○ _____
- ○ _____

What do you have **both** expertise in and interest in, that your ideal audience would love to know more about?

- ○ _____
- ○ _____
- ○ _____
- ○ _____
- ○ _____

Notes: _____

_____

_____

_____

Decide on a Topic for Your Challenge Experience

Today's action step is to choose a topic for your challenge experience. As you decide on challenge topic, draw from the intersection of; your knowledge and expertise, your students' needs, and what you'd enjoy teaching.

Turn to the following page and complete the action steps. What do your students want and what benefits will they receive as a result of participating in your program? Let this guide you as you consider a topic for your challenge.

At the end of the day, journal your accomplishments in the section provided below. By prioritizing time to take action and reflect on your activity and results each day, you'll maximize the benefits you'll receive from this opportunity.

What I Accomplished Today

Activity #5 - Action Steps

Decide on a Topic for Your Challenge Experience

What would you love to teach, based on your expertise? _____

_____

_____

How will your students benefit as a result of participating in your program?

_____

_____

_____

What would you like participants to accomplish by going through your challenge?

_____

_____

_____

Based on your areas of expertise and what your target audience most wants and needs, what topics would you be interested in creating a challenge on? Circle the topic you feel your audience would be **most** interested in.

○ _____

○ _____

○ _____

○ _____

What will be the topic of your challenge? _____

_____

Choose a Name for Your Challenge

Today's action step is to decide on a name for your challenge. Choose one that is clear and that talks about the benefit of your program, to the participant.

The name of your challenge is one of the first things people will see when reading about your program. You want the title to be compelling and attractive to your ideal audience.

Choose a name for your challenge that will attract the right people to your program, like bees to honey.

At the end of the day, journal your accomplishments in the section provided below. By prioritizing time to take action and reflect on your activity and results each day, you'll maximize the benefits you'll receive from this opportunity.

What I Accomplished Today

Activity #6 - Action Steps

Choose a Name for Your Challenge

In one sentence, describe the main benefit of your challenge. _____

_____

_____

List possible titles for your program and check off your top choice.

○ _____

○ _____

○ _____

○ _____

○ _____

The working title of my challenge is: _____

_____

Based on your top choice for a title, compose a couple of possible sub-titles.

○ _____

_____

○ _____

_____

The working subtitle of my challenge is:_____

_____

Notes

Next Steps

_____   _____

_____   _____

_____   _____

_____   _____

_____   _____

_____   _____

_____   _____

_____   _____

_____   _____

_____   _____

_____   _____

_____   _____

Notes

Section Two

Create Your Challenge Road Map and Develop Your Content

Activities 7-14

In this section we'll focus on developing your challenge content. You'll choose the length of your challenge and then outline your modules and action steps.

This will provide you with a road map of your challenge and make it fun and easy for you to develop your program materials.

Activity #7

Record Your Findings from Section One

Today's action step is to review your responses to the exercises in section one. This information will equip you so you can begin to outline your challenge content, training and action steps.

Knowing what your "why" is, who your target audience is, and what solution your audience is seeking will provide you with clarity as to what training and action steps to provide over the course of your challenge. In the process you'll also have the opportunity to decide on your challenge length and whether you'll offer it for free or for a fee.

At the end of the day, journal your accomplishments in the section provided below. By prioritizing time to take action and reflect on your activity and results each day, you'll maximize the benefits you'll receive from this opportunity.

What I Accomplished Today

Activity #7 - Action Steps

Record Your Findings from Section One

What is your "why" for wanting to create a challenge for your audience? _____

_____

_____

Describe your ideal audience? _____

_____

_____

In one sentence, describe the main benefit of your challenge. _____

_____

_____

What is the topic for your challenge? _____

_____

What solution does your challenge solve? _____

_____

_____

What is the title of your challenge? _____

_____

What is the sub-title of your challenge? (optional) _____

_____

Activity #8

Choose Your Challenge Components

Today's action step is to review the challenge components listed on the following page. You'll likely find that ideas spark for you as you look over the possible challenge options, lengths, formats, pricing and more.

Please note that you can be as creative as you'd like as you develop your challenge. You are only limited by your imagination. Refer to the lists on the following page and check off the items that appeal to you or that spark ideas for you. Creating a challenge experience can be a lot of fun for you as well as helpful and enjoyable for your participants.

At the end of the day, journal your accomplishments in the section provided below. By prioritizing time to take action and reflect on your activity and results each day, you'll maximize the benefits you'll receive from this opportunity.

What I Accomplished Today

Activity #8 - Action Steps

Choose Your Challenge Components
Choose All That Apply

Challenge Length	Challenge Pricing
☐ 7 Days ☐ 21 Days ☐ 30 Days ☐ Other:	☐ My challenge will be offered for free as a way to grow my email list. ☐ I plan on charging for my challenge. ☐ Price range I'm considering: $_____
What Your Challenge is Based On	**Challenge Delivery Schedule**
☐ A challenge based on my book. ☐ A challenge based on my knowledge. ☐ A challenge based on my experience. ☐ Other:	☐ Challenge content will be delivered **daily,** via email. ☐ Challenge content will be delivered **weekly**, via email.
Social Interaction	**Challenge Content**
☐ I'd like to have a private Facebook Discussion Forum for my challenge ☐ I will encourage participants to share their comments via my blog posts. ☐ Other:	☐ Content will be delivered exclusively via email. ☐ I would like to offer a weekly call or training session to participants. ☐ I plan on creating handouts, such as worksheets, for my challenge. ☐ Other:
Notes:	Notes

35

Date: _____

Decide on the Length of Your Challenge

Today's action step is to decide on the length of your challenge. You can base this decision on several factors such as your challenge pricing, your goals for challenge and how long it would take for participants to experience results.

It could be that your goal is to offer great content and value while growing your email list, via a free challenge. Or perhaps your goal is to boost your income and attract people who are ready and willing to invest in the solution that your challenge provides. Turn to the following page and complete the exercises, which are designed to help you select the length of your challenge.

At the end of the day, journal your accomplishments in the section provided below. By prioritizing time to take action and reflect on your activity and results each day, you'll maximize the benefits you'll receive from this opportunity.

What I Accomplished Today

Activity #9 - Action Steps

Decide on the Length of Your Challenge

What is your primary goal for your challenge?

- ☐ Grow my email list.
- ☐ Boost my income.

What is your secondary goal for your challenge? (Choose all that apply.)

- ☐ Demonstrate my expertise on a topic.
- ☐ Have people register for a free challenge and then upgrade to a paid program, challenge, or coaching.
- ☐ Connect with people who are willing to invest in receiving a result.

Thoughts to consider in regards to choosing the length of your challenge.

- A short challenge, of 5-7 days, is ideal for a free type of challenge, which you deliver via email or brief videos.
- One of the main goals of a challenge is to grow relationships with members of your community. This is more easily accomplished if you have more time with them. That said, 21 or 30 days would be ideal.
- You can offer a 21 or 30-day challenge for free or for a fee.
- You don't want your challenge to be too long, as people tend to disengage or get distracted.

What are your thoughts regarding how long it will take for participants to experience the results your challenge promises?

_____

_____

What length are you thinking of for your challenge? _____

_____

Choose Your Challenge Modules or Main Topics

Today's action step is to divide your challenge into topics or modules. This helps you as you create the steps for your challenge and it helps your participants as they can more easily digest segmented chunks of content.

When creating a challenge around your book, for example, you can select modules based on chapters or sections. In developing your challenge content, having four or five modules is more manageable and more easily digested, than having a twelve or twenty module program. Keep in mind that you do not have to deliver your entire book or knowledge base in your challenge. Your challenge can lead participants to your book or future programs.

At the end of the day, journal your accomplishments in the section provided below. By prioritizing time to take action and reflect on your activity and results each day, you'll maximize the benefits you'll receive from this opportunity.

What I Accomplished Today

Activity #10 - Action Steps

Choose Your Challenge Modules or Main Topics

My challenge topic or title is: _____

_____

Description of my challenge: _____

_____

_____

My challenge is based on my (book, knowledge, experience.) _____

_____

Keep in mind that there are no hard and fast rules in regards to the focus areas for your challenge. Focus on delivering actionable content that builds on itself.

- For a 7-day challenge, you can share 7 lessons on aspects of one topic.
- For a 21-day challenge, you can easily divide the content into 3 topic areas, delivered over the 3 weeks / 21-days.
- A 30-day challenge can easily be divided into four or give topic areas.

What are the main topics you'd like to include in your challenge? You can base this on steps or chapters/sections of your book, for example.

- O _____
- O _____
- O _____
- O _____
- O _____

Divide Your Modules into Bite-Size Steps

Today's action step is to title your modules and select bullet points to represent the key concepts you'll teach in each module.

Identify the steps you'd like to include in each module. You'll be able to draw from this outline, when we focus on developing the content for each step of your challenge. Print off copies of the following page so you can create an outline for each module of your challenge. **Use the backside of the page if you need room for additional action steps.**

At the end of the day, journal your accomplishments in the section provided below. By prioritizing time to take action and reflect on your activity and results each day, you'll maximize the benefits you'll receive from this opportunity.

What I Accomplished Today

Activity #11 - Action Steps

List Your Module Titles and Break into Action Steps

Module #____ Title: _____

○ _____

○ _____

○ _____

○ _____

○ _____

○ _____

Module #____ Title: _____

○ _____

○ _____

○ _____

○ _____

○ _____

○ _____

Module #____ Title: _____

○ _____

○ _____

○ _____

○ _____

○ _____

○ _____

Print this page multiple times to outline each of your modules.

Date: _____

Describe Each Step of Your Challenge

Today's action step is describe each step of your challenge. By doing so, you'll be prepared to fully develop your challenge content. By seeing your challenge steps written out, you may decide to reorder your steps or add additional steps in order to round out the content.

By writing up a description for each of your steps, you'll also be preparing content which you can use to promote your challenge. This content can be used in email marketing and can be featured on your challenge sales page or registration page.

At the end of the day, journal your accomplishments in the section provided below. By prioritizing time to take action and reflect on your activity and results each day, you'll maximize the benefits you'll receive from this opportunity.

What I Accomplished Today

Activity #12 - Action Steps

Module #____ Action Steps At-a-Glance

Refer to the bulleted lists you created in the previous action step. Plug that information in below and begin to flesh out your challenge content. Print off a copy of this page for each of your modules. Use the back of this page for additional steps.

Module # ____ Module Title:	
Step Number and Title of Activity	**Description of this Step**
Challenge Step #____ Title: _____ _____	Description of this step:
Challenge Step #____ Title: _____ _____	Description of this step:
Challenge Step #____ Title: _____ _____	Description of this step:
Challenge Step #____ Title: _____ _____	Description of this step:
Challenge Step #____ Title: _____ _____	Description of this step:
Challenge Step #____ Title: _____ _____	Description of this step:

Activity #13

Develop Action Steps for Each Challenge Step

Today's activity is to develop action steps for each of your challenge steps. Provide your participants with a way to apply what they've learned, in each step of your challenge. As a rule of thumb, your action steps should be focused and directly related to that day's challenge step, so participants are more likely to complete the activities, rather than wait until they have more time.

When deciding on action steps for each of your challenge steps, keep in mind that "less is more." You want participants to be able to complete the action steps quickly and easily, without getting overwhelmed.

At the end of the day, journal your accomplishments in the section provided below. By prioritizing time to take action and reflect on your activity and results each day, you'll maximize the benefits you'll receive from this opportunity.

What I Accomplished Today

Activity #13 - Action Steps

Develop Action Steps for Module #____

Challenge Step #____ Title: _____ Action Steps:	Challenge Step #____ Title: _____ Action Steps:
Challenge Step #____ Title: _____ Action Steps:	Challenge Step #____ Title: _____ Action Steps:
Challenge Step #____ Title: _____ Action Steps:	Challenge Step #____ Title: _____ Action Steps:

Print this page multiple times and create action steps for each module.
Use the back of the page if you have additional steps in your modules.

Activity #14 Date: _____

Begin to Compose Content for Challenge Steps

Today's action step is to begin to fully develop each of your challenge steps. The most effective way to do this is, one module at a time. Locate your module description page & your action steps page for your each module. Pull from the content on those pages to develop a complete picture for each challenge step in each module. This text is what you will email your challenge participants.

Pace yourself as you compose your challenge content. You may want to set a goal of completing two or three steps per sitting. Then take a break and come back to it, either later that day or during your next scheduled work session.

At the end of the day, journal your accomplishments in the section provided below. By prioritizing time to take action and reflect on your activity and results each day, you'll maximize the benefits you'll receive from this opportunity.

What I Accomplished Today

Activity #14 - Action Steps

Compose the Content for Each Challenge Step

Challenge Step #____ Title: _____

Compose one paragraph introducing this step's topic. _____

_____

_____

_____

_____

Add training tips or additional content. _____

_____

_____

_____

_____

Invite people to participate in activities, such as a Facebook Discussion Forum.

_____

_____

List the Action Steps for This Challenge Step:

Print out a copy of this page for each step of your challenge. Or you can compose your content in a Word document, drawing from the above.

Notes

Next Steps

_____   _____

_____   _____

_____   _____

_____   _____

_____   _____

_____   _____

_____   _____

_____   _____

_____   _____

_____   _____

_____   _____

_____   _____

Notes

Section Three
Design and Deliver Effective Program Materials

Activities
15 - 22

Now that you've outlined your challenge content and action steps, it's time to develop support materials and deliver your challenge content.

In determining the type of support materials you'll deliver, give thought to what would be most useful for your participants.

Challenge Steps and Tasks At-a-Glance

Today's action step is to draw from the activities in the previous section and finish composing content for each challenge step. This content can then be used as the content you send out via email, for each of your challenge steps.

Fill in the Challenge Steps and Tasks worksheet on the following page. Check off that you've created the challenge content and action steps, and have created an email, for each challenge step. This will allow you to check off completed steps and know what tasks still need to be completed. This will prepare you to be able to delivery your challenge to your participants.

At the end of the day, journal your accomplishments in the section provided below. By prioritizing time to take action and reflect on your activity and results each day, you'll maximize the benefits you'll receive from this opportunity.

What I Accomplished Today

Activity #15 - Action Steps

Challenge Steps and Tasks At-a-Glance

Step # ___ Title: _____ ☐Challenge Content ☐Action Steps ☐Email	Step # ___ Title: _____ ☐Challenge Content ☐Action Steps ☐Email
Step # ___ Title: _____ ☐Challenge Content ☐Action Steps ☐Email	Step # ___ Title: _____ ☐Challenge Content ☐Action Steps ☐Email
Step # ___ Title: _____ ☐Challenge Content ☐Action Steps ☐Email	Step # ___ Title: _____ ☐Challenge Content ☐Action Steps ☐Email
Step # ___ Title: _____ ☐Challenge Content ☐Action Steps ☐Email	Step # ___ Title: _____ ☐Challenge Content ☐Action Steps ☐Email
Step # ___ Title: _____ ☐Challenge Content ☐Action Steps ☐Email	Step # ___ Title: _____ ☐Challenge Content ☐Action Steps ☐Email
Step # ___ Title: _____ ☐Challenge Content ☐Action Steps ☐Email	Step # ___ Title: _____ ☐Challenge Content ☐Action Steps ☐Email
Step # ___ Title: _____ ☐Challenge Content ☐Action Steps ☐Email	Step # ___ Title: _____ ☐Challenge Content ☐Action Steps ☐Email
Step # ___ Title: _____ ☐Challenge Content ☐Action Steps ☐Email	Step # ___ Title: _____ ☐Challenge Content ☐Action Steps ☐Email
Step # ___ Title: _____ ☐Challenge Content ☐Action Steps ☐Email	Step # ___ Title: _____ ☐Challenge Content ☐Action Steps ☐Email
Step # ___ Title: _____ ☐Challenge Content ☐Action Steps ☐Email	Step # ___ Title: _____ ☐Challenge Content ☐Action Steps ☐Email
Step # ___ Title: _____ ☐Challenge Content ☐Action Steps ☐Email	Step # ___ Title: _____ ☐Challenge Content ☐Action Steps ☐Email
Step # ___ Title: _____ ☐Challenge Content ☐Action Steps ☐Email	Step # ___ Title: _____ ☐Challenge Content ☐Action Steps ☐Email
Step # ___ Title: _____ ☐Challenge Content ☐Action Steps ☐Email	Step # ___ Title: _____ ☐Challenge Content ☐Action Steps ☐Email
Step # ___ Title: _____ ☐Challenge Content ☐Action Steps ☐Email	Step # ___ Title: _____ ☐Challenge Content ☐Action Steps ☐Email
Step # ___ Title: _____ ☐Challenge Content ☐Action Steps ☐Email	Step # ___ Title: _____ ☐Challenge Content ☐Action ☐Email

Activity #16

Create Challenge Worksheets and Materials

Today's action step is to begin to create support materials for your challenge steps. From worksheets, to checklists, to PDF versions of your challenge steps, there are a variety of support materials you can provide to participants.

Go through your challenge steps, one at a time, and review the training and action steps you've identified. Next, develop support materials, such as tracking sheets, checklists, and worksheets, to help participants capture ideas, check off their accomplishments and track their activity and their results.

At the end of the day, journal your accomplishments in the section provided below. By prioritizing time to take action and reflect on your activity and results each day, you'll maximize the benefits you'll receive from this opportunity.

What I Accomplished Today

Activity #16 - Action Steps

Create Challenge Worksheets and Materials

Here are some ideas to draw from as you give thought to the types of support materials you'd like to offer your challenge participants.

Option One: Create a variety of materials for your challenge steps.

Are you taking participants through a step by step process (as we are in this program) that requires them to complete activities that build on one another? If so, you'll want to develop support materials that equips them in completing tasks and recording their activities and results.

Option Two: Create a simple daily or weekly tracking sheet that is used to record activity and results, for each step of your challenge. Each time you send out a new challenge step via email, you can include a link to the PDF version of the "Daily Tracking Sheet."

This option is perfect for challenges that encourage participants to develop new habits. In essence, you are using the same tracking sheet for each step.

Some examples of this are:

- ☐ Healthy habits challenges
- ☐ Relationship based challenges
- ☐ Behavioral based challenges
- ☐ Marketing activities challenges
- ☐ Other: _____

View the following pages for examples of handouts that participants could use for each step of a challenge experience. Draw from these examples and give thought to what activities you'll want your participants to record.

55

My Daily Challenge Journal

Challenge Day # _____   Day & Date: _____

What I did to (challenge topic) _____ today:

_____

_____

Tactics that are working: _____

_____

_____

Results I am experiencing: _____

_____

_____

What I'm grateful for today: _____

_____

_____

Notes:

Tracking My Daily Healthy Habits for the Week of: _____

These are the healthy habits I am tracking as part of this challenge.

Healthy Habits Tracking	M	T	W	T	F	S	S

My End of the Week Review

Something wonderful that happened this week: _____

_____

_____

What I'm most excited about having accomplished this week: _____

_____

_____

What I'll do to celebrate my accomplishments: _____

_____

_____

What I'm most grateful for: _____

_____

_____

Date: _____

Brainstorm Ideas for Your Challenge Handouts

Today's action step is to begin to design and create your challenge handouts. Turn to the following page and begin to brainstorm and develop ideas for your challenge handouts.

While you don't have to provide handouts for your challenge, they do help to anchor students to the content and provide them with a way to chart their journey and keep track of their activities and results. Have fun with this exercise and know that you can always revise content as you go along.

At the end of the day, journal your accomplishments in the section provided below. By prioritizing time to take action and reflect on your activity and results each day, you'll maximize the benefits you'll receive from this opportunity.

What I Accomplished Today

Activity #17 - Action Steps

Brainstorm Ideas for Your Challenge Handouts

Which best describes your challenge experience?

- ☐ My challenge participants will be developing new habits. I **do not** need a different worksheet for each challenge step. Participants can print off multiple copies of daily or weekly tracking sheets to track their progress.

- ☐ My challenge participants will receive step-by-step training on a specific topic along with action steps that help them to take action on what they learn.

- ☐ Other: _____

_____

_____

Which types of handouts would you like to offer (check all that apply.)

- ☐ I'd like to offer a daily tracking sheet.
- ☐ I'd like to offer a weekly tracking sheet.
- ☐ I'd like to offer a PDF copy of each challenge step.
- ☐ I'd like to offer tracking sheets that support specific challenge steps.

Notes: _____

_____

_____

_____

_____

Activity #18   Date: _____

Preparing Your Handouts for Delivery

Today's action step is to prepare your challenge handouts for delivery. Handouts can be created using software programs such as Microsoft PowerPoint or Word. These programs provide you with the opportunity to save a document in PDF format. This format is extremely user-friendly.

Once documents have been saved in PDF format, they can be uploaded to your website or online storage facility. You can then copy the URL to the files and paste them into email messages. This method of document delivery is preferred over sending documents as attachments.

At the end of the day, journal your accomplishments in the section provided below. By prioritizing time to take action and reflect on your activity and results each day, you'll maximize the benefits you'll receive from this opportunity.

What I Accomplished Today

Activity #18 - Action Steps
Preparing Your Handouts for Delivery

When creating your handouts, there are a few things you can do to make them as attractive and inviting as possibly.

- ○ Label your handouts with clear titles.
- ○ Include clear and concise instructions.
- ○ Write brief paragraphs and leave whitespace between paragraphs.
- ○ Include checklists or bulleted action steps that participants can check off as they gather information and complete tasks and activities.
- ○ Provide lined sections where participants can record their ideas.
- ○ You can also add your branding to the bottom of each page if you'd like.

Instructions for Uploading and Saving Your Document in PDF Format

1. Create your handouts using a program such as PowerPoint or Word.

2. Save your file in PDF format. For example, in PowerPoint or Word you can:

   - Click on the "edit" tab at the top of the screen and select "save as."

   - Save as a PDF file and save to a dedicated file folder on your computer.

3. Upload the PDF to your website. In WordPress for example:

   - Go to your WordPress dashboard and click on the "media" tab.

   - Upload the PDF file to your media library. Once uploaded click on the "edit" tab to access the link to the PDF file.

   - This is the URL you paste into an email when delivering your content.

4. The reason you post a link to the PDF rather than send it as an email attachment, is that many people will not open email attachments. You want to make it as easy for people to access your materials.

Date: _____

Deliver Your Challenge Content via Email

Today's action step is to set up a way to deliver your challenge steps via email. To do this you'll want to use an email service that allows you to send auto-responder messages. An auto-responder provides you with a way to schedule emails to go out automatically.

They are designed so that when someone registers for your program, they receive the first message. They'll then receive other messages in the series, based on the delivery schedule you've set up. This will keep your students engaged while providing them with easy access to the challenge content.

At the end of the day, journal your accomplishments in the section provided below. By prioritizing time to take action and reflect on your activity and results each day, you'll maximize the benefits you'll receive from this opportunity.

What I Accomplished Today

Activity #19 - Action Steps

Delivering Your Challenge Content via Email

Anatomy of a Challenge Email Message for Your Auto-Responder Series

Email Subject Line: Choose 1-2 words that you'll use at the beginning of each challenge message, so your students can easily locate these messages. As an example you could use something like [Author Challenge] in the subject lines.

Personalized Greeting: Most email service providers, such as AWeber, provide you with a way to personalize your messages by adding your students' names to the subject lines and the body of the messages. This adds a nice touch and increases the odds of recipients opening your email and taking action.

Create a consistent formula for your challenge email messages so your students know that to expect. Be sure to use white space between paragraphs.

Here's an example that you can draw from:

- List the number and name of the challenge step they're receiving that day.
- Compose a brief paragraph describing what they'll be learning.
- Share additional content as applicable.
- Include one or a few action steps that help them apply what they learn.
- Paste the link to that challenge step's worksheets, if applicable.
- Provide them with a link to your Facebook group, if applicable.
- End the email as you would end a letter to a friend, and add your name.

Resources:

- AWeber: WebMailConnections.com
- MailChimp: MailChimp.com

Activity #20   Date: _____

Provide Interaction via a Facebook Group

Today's action step is to set up your Facebook Group for your program. A Facebook group can serve as a discussion forum and create wonderful opportunities for interaction.

Participants will benefit from being able to connect with others who are interested in the topic of your challenge. Your Facebook group also provides you with the ability to easily answer questions that can benefit the person asking the question as well as the entire group.

At the end of the day, journal your accomplishments in the section provided below. By prioritizing time to take action and reflect on your activity and results each day, you'll maximize the benefits you'll receive from this opportunity.

What I Accomplished Today

Activity #20 - Action Steps

Provide Interaction via a Facebook Group

Having a Facebook group provides an easy way for you to: connect with participants, answer questions, post announcements, and deliver great value.

Instructions for setting up a Facebook group.

- ○ To create a Facebook group, login to Facebook and go to your "home" tab.
- ○ From your home tab, look for the word "groups" at the far left of the page.
- ○ Click on "groups" and then look for a "create a group" button at the top right of the page. You'll then be guided through the process.
- ○ As you set up your group, give strategic thought to what you want to call it. Popular options include, your company or brand name, your program name, or an umbrella name that can apply to future programs you offer.
- ○ Brand your group by adding a cover image at the top of the page. You'll see an image of a camera in that area. When you hover over it you'll see the option to "change cover image."
- ○ An easy way to create a cover image for your group is via Canva.com. Set up a free Canva account then look for the Facebook template. Click on it and have fun as you add your branded colors and group name.

Once your group is set up, it's time to invite people to join in the conversation. Include an invitation and a link to your group, in each email that you send out to your challenge participants. Here are some tips for creating engagement:

- ○ Post a welcoming message and invite people to introduce themselves.
- ○ Mention that the group is a great place to share successes & ask questions.
- ○ Add conversation starters and ask thought-provoking questions.
- ○ Participants will begin interacting and starting new conversations.

Activity #21   Date: _____

Deliver Challenge Content via a Facebook Group

Today's action step is to explore the option for delivering your challenge content via your Facebook group. The benefits of this are, that participants will have an easy way to access all of the challenge steps in one handy location. You still may want to deliver your content via email though as not everyone checks their Facebook messages as often as they check their email messages.

When people join your Facebook group, you can warmly invite them to join in the conversation and let them know that they can access each of the challenge steps via the "files" tab in the group.

At the end of the day, journal your accomplishments in the section provided below. By prioritizing time to take action and reflect on your activity and results each day, you'll maximize the benefits you'll receive from this opportunity.

What I Accomplished Today

Activity #21 - Action Steps

Deliver Challenge Content via a Facebook Group

Things to consider when uploading your challenge content to Facebook.

- ☐ When uploading content to Facebook, you want to upload PDF files and not editable files, such as PowerPoint or Word files.

- ☐ You can post links to your conference calls and replays via the "files" tab.

- ☐ Decide if you'll be delivering the content in real time, so your initial participants receive access to steps, one step at a time, as you go along.

- ☐ Moving forward, if all of your steps are available via a Facebook group, are you okay with participants having access to all of the content?

- ☐ If you are providing access to all of the content at once, you may want to post a sentence on your registration page that let's people know that there are no refunds as they receive instant access to the entire program.

To add a file to your group:

- Login to Facebook and go to your group.
- Compose a message describing the file.
- You'll see "more" drop down menu just above the message.
- Select the option to upload a file.
- Once you've done this the first time, a "files" tab will appear at the top of your group page.
- Moving forward you can click directly on the files tab to add new files.

What are your thoughts regarding uploading challenge steps to your group?

_____

_____

_____

Activity #22   Date: _____

Enhance Your Program with Conference Calls

Today's action step is to explore the possibility of adding conference calls to your challenge experience. Conference calls are easy to conduct and they provide you with a wonderful way to enhance your program and connect with your participants.

If your program is divided into modules, for example, you could offer a weekly training call and/or question and answer call. Perhaps you'd like to offer the conference call option seasonally or just during the first run of your program. Conference calls can add great value to your program.

At the end of the day, journal your accomplishments in the section provided below. By prioritizing time to take action and reflect on your activity and results each day, you'll maximize the benefits you'll receive from this opportunity.

What I Accomplished Today

Activity #22 - Action Steps

Enhance Your Program with Conference Calls

Conference calls are easy to conduct and can be quite enjoyable. Here are a few tips as well as some food for thought.

- ○ Conference calls add great value to your program. You can expand on challenge content and provide a way for participants to ask questions.

- ○ Providing ways for your audience to connect with you and hear your voice will increase your credibility and your bond with your audience.

- ○ Your challenge program can be offered year round, with the content delivered on auto-pilot.

- ○ You may want to roll out a "live" version of your program one or more times a year. You can then offer conference calls at those times.

- ○ If you find that your program is bringing in a fair number of enrollments on a regular basis, you could consider offering weekly or monthly calls.

What are your thoughts about adding conference calls to your challenge?

- ○ _____
- ○ _____
- ○ _____
- ○ _____
- ○ _____

Resources:

- • WebTeleseminars.com - For calls and web based audio. You can even add PowerPoint slides if you'd like to add in a visual component.

- • FreeConferenceCalling.com - For U.S. based calls.

- • FreeConferenceCall.com - For International calls.

Notes

Next Steps

_____   _____

_____   _____

_____   _____

_____   _____

_____   _____

_____   _____

_____   _____

_____   _____

_____   _____

_____   _____

_____   _____

_____   _____

Notes

Section Four

Market and Launch Your Challenge

Activities 23-30

The next step on your challenge creation journey is to compose promotional content to help you market and launch your program.

You also need a way for participants to register for your program. In this section you'll discover simple solutions for achieving the above.

Create a Sales Page So Participants Can Register

Today's action step is to create a sales page for your challenge. A sales page is where people go to find out about and register for your course.

You can post your sales page as a fresh page on your website or you can use a sales page template using a WordPress plugin such as Thrive Themes Content Builder. (ReachMoreReaders.com/thrivethemes)

Another option is to offer your challenge via an online classroom platform, such as CourseCraft.net and post your sales page there.

At the end of the day, journal your accomplishments in the section provided below. By prioritizing time to take action and reflect on your activity and results each day, you'll maximize the benefits you'll receive from this opportunity.

What I Accomplished Today

Activity #23 - Action Steps
Create a Sales Page for Your Challenge

Your sales page provides a way for people to find out about and register for your challenge. The words written on the page, known as *copy*, should focus on the challenges your students face along with the benefits your program offers.

Anatomy of a Sales Page - Turn the page for a fill-in-the blanks template

- ☐ Compose a benefit driven title, which goes at the top of the page.

- ☐ Add an emotion provoking subtitle, such as a question, that allows readers to get in touch with their pain.

- ☐ Add a paragraphs that acknowledge the reader's challenge.

- ☐ Paint the picture of how things could be better.

- ☐ Describe what your challenge experience can offer, focusing on how they'll benefit by going through your program. (Focus on the benefits to the students and what they'll gain and not what stuff they'll receive.)

- ☐ Include a benefit driven title and a few benefit driven bullet points for each module in your program. (Example: Rather than saying, you'll learn how to set up your website, say something like: Discover how to create a magnetic book blog, that will keep visitors coming back time after time.)

- ☐ Include student, client, and/or colleague testimonials.

- ☐ Add a way for students to pay for or register for your challenge.

- ☐ Decide on pricing and set up a buy button. (You can either add a PayPal button to your website or, if you're registering students through CourseCraft (for example) they'll walk you through the process.

Map Out the Content for Your Sales Page

Compose a benefit driven title, which goes at the top of the page: _____

_____

Add an emotion provoking subtitle, such as a question, that allows readers to get in touch with their pain: _____

_____

Add a paragraph that acknowledges their challenge:_____

_____

_____

_____

Describe what your program can offer your students, focusing on how they'll benefit by going through your program. Focus on the benefits to the students and what they'll gain rather than the "stuff" they'll receive.

_____

_____

_____

Collect testimonials from students, clients, and colleagues. Whenever someone complements you on your program or work, thank them & ask if you can share their comment as a testimonial. Open up a Word document and begin to collect testimonials. Post one of your favorite testimonials in the space provided below.

_____

Talk About Benefits Rather Than Features

Provide a module by module outline of your program. Rather than list the title and the concepts they'll learn, compose text that focuses on the benefits they'll receive from each module. On your sales page, include benefit driven titles and a few benefit driven bullet points for each module in your program.

Transform your module titles and key concepts into benefit driven statements:

Module: _____

  Benefit: _____

  Benefit: _____

  Benefit: _____

Module: _____

  Benefit: _____

  Benefit: _____

  Benefit: _____

Module: _____

  Benefit: _____

  Benefit: _____

  Benefit: _____

Module: _____

  Benefit: _____

  Benefit: _____

  Benefit: _____

Module: _____

  Benefit: _____

  Benefit: _____

  Benefit: _____

Activity #24   Date: _____

Add a Buy Button to Your Sales Page

Today's action step is to set up a buy button on your sales page. This is what your challenge participants will click on in order to pay to participate in your challenge.

When offering a free challenge, students will register by subscribing to your email list, as discussed in the previous section. In order to participate in a fee based challenge, students will need to have a way to pay for your program. Turn to the following page for instructions on setting up a buy button. You can also search YouTube for a tutorial on "setting up a PayPal buy button."

At the end of the day, journal your accomplishments in the section provided below. By prioritizing time to take action and reflect on your activity and results each day, you'll maximize the benefits you'll receive from this opportunity.

What I Accomplished Today

Activity #24 - Action Steps

Set Up a PayPal Buy Button on Your Sales Page

Provide your challenge participants with a way to pay for your program. PayPal offers a popular and simple solution. You can set up a buy button directly through PayPal, or you can link your PayPal account to an online classroom platform, such as CourseCraft.net. This will also get students onto your email list. You can register for a free account or upgrade your challenge to the pro level.

Following are the steps for setting up a buy button via your PayPal account.

Step One: Login or register for a PayPal account.

Step Two: Locate the PayPal Buttons section. While PayPal updates their site interface from time to time, you can currently locate the PayPal buttons section by clicking on the "Tools" tab at the top of your PayPal dashboard. From there, click on "More Tools" then scroll down to the box labeled "PayPal Buttons."

Step Three: Next, click the text that says "create new button" and fill in the relevant fields on the form. The screens walk you through the process. Once you fill in all the form data, click save. You'll then have the options to copy the HTML button code to paste to your sales page, or the Email URL, which you can hyperlink to a payment button image that you upload to your sales page.

Take note that:

○ A "buy" button is for a one-time purchase and a "subscribe" button is for multi-pay or monthly payment plan options.

○ In step 3 on the PayPal button form you can paste the URL to a thank you page. This is important as you will want to provide instructions.

○ PayPal will not add people to your email list. Have a note that says to "register your name and email address in order to receive access to the challenge materials." Below that message post an opt-in form that will add students to your challenge email list.

Activity #25

Craft Marketing Emails to Promote the Challenge

Today's action step is to compose email messages that educate your email subscribers as well as messages that directly market your challenge.

Your email list is comprised of members of your target audience who have indicated that they are interested in what you have to say. Provide valuable and interesting content to your list on your topic area. This will also provide you with the opportunity to promote your challenge to them. Take care to focus on building relationships and sharing value. Then, when you go to market your challenge, people will see this as another way to learn from you.

At the end of the day, journal your accomplishments in the section provided below. By prioritizing time to take action and reflect on your activity and results each day, you'll maximize the benefits you'll receive from this opportunity.

What I Accomplished Today

Activity #25 - Action Steps
Prepare Your Marketing Messages

Email marketing is a mix of providing education and inspiration along with opportunities for people to invest in resources that support their goals.

Email services such as AWeber, allow you to create multiple lists. You an have one list that markets to subscribers and another that provides your challenge members with access to your challenge materials. You can even set up an email automation rule that unsubscribes people from the marketing list when they register for your paid program. Refer to your email services tutorials for details.

Create a set of emails that are designed to educate your subscribers.

- Use compelling subject lines that will entice your subscribers.

- Begin your email with a warm welcome or friendly greeting.

- Tell a short story or share something you recently learned, based on the topic of your email message.

- Keep paragraphs short and leave white space between paragraphs.

- Tie email messages to the topic of to your challenge.

- Include an invitation to register for your challenge.

- Focus on the actual benefits students will receive by participating in your challenge rather than the program features or stuff they'll get.

- Include testimonials in some of your messages.

- Provide a call-to-action and invite them to register.

Turn the page and complete the exercises for outlining a series of educational emails as well as a series of promotional emails.

Crafting Your Email Subject Lines

The most important aspect of an email is the subject line. Your subject line is what determines whether or not people open your emails. When composing email subject lines, use words that will intrigue your readers.

Create a list of topics you could write about, related to your challenge:

_____

_____

_____

_____

Transform this list of topics into subject lines for educational emails:

_____

_____

_____

_____

You'll also want to create subject lines that directly promote your challenge:

_____

_____

_____

Create an Outline with Ideas for Your Emails

Use the space below to brainstorm ideas for your educational emails and your marketing emails. Then, open up a Word document, compose your messages, and save them to your computer.

Hot Tip: Always reread what you've composed, putting yourself in the shoes of your subscribers, before sending out an email.

Notes for Email Message #1

_____

_____

_____

_____

_____

_____

Notes for Email Message #2

_____

_____

_____

_____

_____

_____

Notes for Email Message #3

_____

_____

_____

_____

_____

Notes for Email Message #4

_____

_____

_____

_____

_____

Activity #26 Date: _____

Grow Your Email List & Challenge Registrations

Today's action step is to find ways to grow the size of your email list. The more people you have on your email list, the more people you'll have register for your programs.

You can grow your list by offering a free level of your challenge or by offering another type of lead magnet. Lead magnets are tools or resources, typically in PDF format, that your ideal audience would love to have! Lead magnets are also referred to as gifts or giveaways. Checklists, worksheets, and top tips lists make wonderful giveaways.

At the end of the day, journal your accomplishments in the section provided below. By prioritizing time to take action and reflect on your activity and results each day, you'll maximize the benefits you'll receive from this opportunity.

What I Accomplished Today

Activity #26 - Action Steps

Grow Your List Size and Challenge Registrations

The easiest way to create a downloadable opt-in gift for your audience is to compose your content in a Word document and then save it to PDF format.

Another option is to offer a free level of your challenge. Which option best describes what you'd like to offer to subscribers?

- ☐ I'd like to offer a free version of my challenge, and will proceed as instructed in previous sections of this workbook.
- ☐ In order to grow my email list, I'd like to offer some sort of downloadable PDF document. (I'll complete the worksheet below to identify an option.)

When creating a downloadable opt-in gift (lead magnet) you want your gift to be on a subject that is of great interest to your niche audience. People love checklists, top tips lists, and worksheets.

Here are some great idea joggers for an opt-in gift:

- ○ Five Top Tops to…
- ○ 7 Ways to …
- ○ Fast Easy Recipes You Can Make in Fifteen Minutes
- ○ Take Action Checklists to Help You...
- ○ Other: _____

In the space below, jot down your ideas for a gift you could create:

_____

_____

_____

Activity #27 Date: _____

Create a Hidden Download Page

Today's action step is to create a hidden download page so you can easily deliver your opt-in gift. You need to have a way for your subscribers to receive their gift. Rather than giving them the link to the PDF file itself, it is more effective to post the download link on a hidden page on your blog.

A hidden page simply means that the name of the page does not show up in your site's navigation menu. Once someone subscribes to your email list, you can have your email system programed to automatically send out a thank you email, which includes a link to your hidden download page.

At the end of the day, journal your accomplishments in the section provided below. By prioritizing time to take action and reflect on your activity and results each day, you'll maximize the benefits you'll receive from this opportunity.

What I Accomplished Today

Activity #27 - Action Steps

Create a Hidden Download Page and Thank You Message

Creating a hidden thank you page is a great way to deliver your opt-in gift. That way, instead of simply getting access to the file, your subscribers will find themselves on your blog. Once they download their gift, they will likely explore your site, to find out more about you and your offerings.

Here's how to create a hidden download page and thank you message:

- ☐ Create a thank you page on your blog and upload your PDF gift.
- ☐ Include text on the page, thanking your subscribers and letting them know to click on the link to access their gift.
- ☐ Copy the URL to the PDF and then hyperlink the text on the page that says something like, "click here to access your gift."
- ☐ If you'd like, you can also invite subscribers to explore your site, or check out your book or challenge, for even more information on the topic.
- ☐ Publish this page as a hidden page (meaning the page title doesn't show up on your site's navigation menu.)
- ☐ Go to your email service and create a thank you follow up message that includes the URL to the hidden page where readers can access your gift.
- ☐ Set this to automatically go out when someone subscribes.

Sample email template for your follow up email:

Hi [Add the short code, from your email service, for their first name]
Thank you for requesting your special gift of: _____
To claim your gift head over to: www._____
I look forward to getting to know you and welcome your questions.
To your success,
[Your Name]

Grow Your Email List Through Online Speaking

Today's action step is to explore the possibilities that online speaking offers. Online speaking can provide you with wonderful exposure and opportunities to connect with your listeners and grow your list of email subscribers.

By being a guest speaker, you'll be able to reach more people in your target audience and increase your visibility. Online interviews are fun and easy to record, and are easily accessible to your audience. By being a guest on interviews, you don't have to worry about any technology, as your host takes care of that from their end.

At the end of the day, journal your accomplishments in the section provided below. By prioritizing time to take action and reflect on your activity and results each day, you'll maximize the benefits you'll receive from this opportunity.

What I Accomplished Today

Activity #28 - Action Steps

Grow Your Email List Through Online Speaking

- ○ Online interviews provide a wonderful platform for promoting your book brand, and challenge, while getting introduced to new audiences.

- ○ Providing ways for your audience to hear you speak on the topic of your challenge, will increase your list size and your program registrations.

- ○ By being a guest speaker on podcasts and Internet radio shows, you'll connect with leaders in your field and increase your credibility.

- ○ By being a guest speaker, you are being endorsed by your hosts and giving listeners the opportunity to get to know you.

- ○ Participating in online interviews—or talking about your challenge topic over the air waves—is a powerful way for your audience to hear your voice and connect with you.

- ○ Online interviews provide you with a way to share your brilliance and your experience with people interested in your topic area.

- ○ In addition to your live interviews, the audio recordings can be made available for people to listen to at their convenience.

When getting interviewed, you often have the opportunity to present the host with a list of questions you'd like to be asked. Without being self-promotional, focus on questions that shine the light on your expertise and challenge topic.

Compose a list of possible interview questions.

- ○ _____
- ○ _____
- ○ _____
- ○ _____
- ○ _____

Locate Online Speaking Opportunities

The easiest way to get started with online speaking is to get interviewed by people you already know, who attract members of your target audience. Once the interview has concluded, be sure to thank your hosts and ask them for referrals to others who interview, in your niche.

Make a list of people you know, or listen to, who have a Podcast or Radio Show

Name of Host	Name of Show or Podcast	Website Address
_____	_____	_____
_____	_____	_____
_____	_____	_____
_____	_____	_____

When searching for shows and podcasts, focus on ones that attract your ideal listener. Compose a list of keywords, or keyword phrases, your audience would type into Google when seeking information on the topic of your challenge.

_____	_____
_____	_____
_____	_____

Use your keywords to locate additional online speaking opportunities. Go to iTunes and BlogTalkRadio.com and search for hosts and shows on your topic.

Name of Host	Name of Show or Podcast	Website Address
_____	_____	_____
_____	_____	_____
_____	_____	_____
_____	_____	_____

Craft Your Speaker Introduction

Use the following template to compose your speaker introduction. This is a great way to shine the spotlight on your expertise. Strive to keep your bio to 100-125 words, unless your host indicates otherwise. This way you'll focus on what's essential and will retain the attention of your listeners.

(Name)_____ of (URL) www._____

is the (author of or expert on): _____.

(One sentence that describe your experience) _____

_____

(One sentence that describes what "you do" or how you help people) _____

_____.

Today (name) will be speaking to us about: _____.

Draw from the above outline to compose your speaker bio: _____

_____

_____

_____

Hot Tip: Typically, at the end of an interview, the host will ask you to let people know the best way to get in touch with you. Rather than giving your listeners multiple options, give them one URL so they take action.

The most effective option is to let them know, with your host's permission, that you have a special gift for them, which they can receive by going to your blog. Provide them with the URL to where they go to register their name and email address in exchange for your gift. This will get them onto your email list.

You'll then have the opportunity to build ongoing relationships with your new subscribers.

Date: _____

Test to Make Sure All Systems Are Go

Today's action step is to make sure all of your systems are in place and then test those systems, before inviting students to join your challenge. There are many moving parts involved when setting up a challenge experience.

Once you are sure that everything is in working order, you'll want to log out of all your accounts and websites and go through the registration process as if you were a new student. If you find something that needs adjusting, make the adjustment, then logout and try it again.

At the end of the day, journal your accomplishments in the section provided below. By prioritizing time to take action and reflect on your activity and results each day, you'll maximize the benefits you'll receive from this opportunity.

What I Accomplished Today

Activity #29 - Action Steps

Test to Make Sure All Systems Are Go

It is essential that you test all of your systems to make sure everything is in place, before inviting people to join your program. Refer to the following checklist to help you with this process.

- ☐ Create your challenge content.
- ☐ Upload your challenge content to your auto-responder service.
- ☐ Set up your auto-responder and schedule your emails for delivery.
- ☐ Set up your Facebook group and add links to your email messages.

- ☐ Create your registration page (for a free challenge.)
- ☐ Create a sales page (for a paid challenge.)
- ☐ Set up your challenge payment button.

- ☐ Select the date your challenge will begin on.
- ☐ Compose your marketing messages and market to your email list.
- ☐ Locate online speaking opportunities and line up some interviews.

- ☐ Register for your program and make sure all systems are go.
- ☐ Note: When registering for a paid challenge, you may need to register via a PayPal account other than your own or test via the "sandbox" setting. Set the test price to $1 and then set the price back once you've registered.
- ☐ Check to see that you received the automated email for your challenge.
- ☐ Once all systems are go, invite people to register for your challenge!

Activity #30

Date: _____

Celebrate and Keep the Momentum Going

Today's action step is to celebrate your accomplishments and put a plan in place to keep your momentum going. Open up your calendar and schedule times to complete, market, and conduct your challenge.

Congratulations, you made it! But, the journey doesn't end here. You'll want to put a plan in place to keep your momentum going. Wherever you are on the spectrum, from brainstorming ideas to conducting your challenge, you are only a decision away from opening up the doors for registration to your challenge. Just think of the positive impact you can have on the lives of others!

At the end of the day, journal your accomplishments in the section provided below. By prioritizing time to take action and reflect on your activity and results each day, you'll maximize the benefits you'll receive from this opportunity.

What I Accomplished Today

Activity #30 - Action Steps

Time to Celebrate and Keep the Momentum Going

Wherever you are, in the process of planning, marketing or conducting your challenge, you are in the perfect place! The key is to keep the momentum going and celebrate your accomplishments along the way. Complete this worksheet and schedule time to keep the ball rolling forward.

Where I am at in regards to preparing, marketing and conducting my challenge:

○ _____

○ _____

○ _____

What I've accomplished so far:

○ _____

○ _____

○ _____

What I will do to celebrate my accomplishments:

○ _____

○ _____

○ _____

What my next steps are:

○ _____

○ _____

○ _____

Notes

Next Steps

_____   _____

_____   _____

_____   _____

_____   _____

_____   _____

_____   _____

_____   _____

_____   _____

_____   _____

_____   _____

_____   _____

_____   _____

Reflections and Next Steps Tracking Sheet

Wherever you are, in the process of planning, marketing or conducting your challenge, you are in the perfect place! The key is to keep the momentum going and celebrate along the way! Fill in your responses below.

Realizations I've had as I've gone through the Create a Challenge action steps:

_____

_____

_____

Any limiting beliefs that are holding me back from creating my challenge:

_____

_____

_____

The main thing I need to do in order to keep moving forward:

_____

_____

_____

Based on where I'm at on this create-a-challenge journey, my next steps are:

○ _____

○ _____

○ _____

○ _____

○ _____

Take Your Learning Further

Register for the Online Training Program and Create a Challenge Experience for Your Audience

Offering a challenge experience to your audience will provide you with many benefits! You'll be able to grow your list of email subscribers, boost your book and product sales and develop relationships with members of your audience.

- ○ Join D'vorah and a group of success-focused authors and entrepreneurs for an interactive, power-packed experience!

- ○ In this program you'll learn how to design, create and market a 30-day challenge, based on your book, knowledge or area of expertise.

- ○ Enjoy hands-on training, step-by-step instruction, group interaction and personalized support in a safe and nurturing environment.

By participating in this program you'll receive:

- ✓ Weekly tutorials that walk you through the process, step-by-step.
- ✓ Access to an interactive discussion forum, where you'll be able to connect with other participants and get your questions answered!
- ✓ A personalized action plan, created by you, for you, that will allow you to create the ideal challenge experience for your audience.

What Type of Impact Would it Have on Your Business and Your Life, to be Able to Offer a Challenge Experience to Your Audience?

This program is available on-demand so there are no dates to worry about. For details about the *Create a Challenge Experience* program go to:

CreateAChallengeExperience.com

About D'vorah

D'vorah Lansky, M.Ed., is the bestselling author of many books including; the *Action Guides for Authors* series of workbooks and journals.

Since 2007 she has created over 25 online training programs and has taught online book marketing strategies to thousands of authors across the globe.

D'vorah specializes in helping authors to build a business around their books, as they grow their reach and share their message with the world.

90 Day Power Plan

90 Days Will Come and Go... Where Will You Be?

The *90 Day Power Plan Take Action Planner* provides you with a tool to help you turbocharge your activity and results. Over the course of 90 days, you'll be able to:

- 📖 Map out an action plan that will allow you to develop new success habits.

- 📖 Effectively track your activity and results so you can become more productive.

- 📖 Focus on what's most essential while making time to enjoy life.

In this 90-day planner you have the opportunity to map out an action plan and record your activity and results. Use this planner to help you set, achieve, and celebrate your weekly, monthly, and 90-day goals.

Available on Amazon or a bookstore near you!
ISBN: 978-0996743198

Action Guides for Authors

These take-action workbooks and journals are designed to help you track your activities and results so you can reach more readers and sell more books.

ActionGuidesForAuthors.com

The Busy Author's Journal Series

The Busy Author's Journal series provides you with 30-day journals designed to help you monitor and track your daily activities and your results. By doing something, even something small each day, you will make a huge splash as you reach more readers, sell more books, and help more people.

The 30 Day Challenge for Authors Series

In the *30 Day Challenge for Authors* series, you have access to step-by-step training and action steps to help you accomplish the tasks laid out in each guide. Over the course of 30 days, you'll be taken on a guided journey and provided with bite-sized activities which will allow you to fit the pieces of the jigsaw puzzle in place.

Available on Amazon at BooksByDvorah.com

www.ingramcontent.com/pod-product-compliance
Lightning Source LLC
Chambersburg PA
CBHW082111070326
40689CB00052B/4502